Pockets of Joy
Journal

With an Introduction by

ROXANE BATTLE

ISBN 13: 978-1-59298-848-8

Library of Congress Catalog Number: 2015913315

Printed in the United States of America

First Printing: 2015

22 21 20 19   5 4 3 2

Edited by Hanna Kjeldbjerg.
Cover and interior design by Laura Drew.

Beaver's Pond Press
7108 Ohms Lane
Edina, MN 55439–2129
952-829-8818
www.beaverspondpress.com

BEAVER'S POND
PRESS

Credits

*Dedicated to any and everyone
brave enough to believe in the prospect of joy.*

Though you have not seen him, you love him;
and even though you do not see him now, you believe in him
and are filled with an inexpressible and glorious joy.

1 Peter 1:8 (NIV)

INTRODUCTION

I BELIEVE THE EXISTENCE OF JOY, JUST LIKE GOD, is ever present.

While it's true that no one has ever seen God, we've all seen panting puppies and laughing babies and their millions of YouTube hits, which proves that joy can erupt all around us, spontaneously, unmanufactured, and void of pretense. Like our reaction to a surprise, a funny joke, or a hummingbird sighting, joy can, and does, just happen. It's real and it can't be faked.

Joy is authenticity amid the banality of life. Joy interrupts our daily routine comprised of errands, checkout lanes, traffic jams, and the sterile smell of the doctor's office. More often than we think or allow ourselves to see, mundane daily living can be interposed with tiny unexpected eruptions—and sometimes even big splashes—of joy. Yet our boredom, our pain, our disappointment, and our anxiety over the next thing we need to do take precedent, and we miss it.

Last summer, I got up early on a Saturday morning to go to the farmers' market, one of my absolute favorite things to do. I was looking forward to walking among the rows of flowers and fresh vegetables, drinking coffee, and doing business with the merchants. Yet on this particular morning, it was cloudy and overcast, and a steady light drizzle was falling. Who wants to go to the farmers' market in the rain? Half the fun was being outside in morning sun among crowds of shoppers hunting for bargains. I was tempted to go back to bed. *Perfect morning for sleeping in,* I rationalized.

Instead, I put on a hat, found my umbrella, and went anyway. The light rain had kept people away, so the market was far less crowded than usual. I walked among the rows and rows of flowers and tables of neatly displayed picked vegetables, chatted with merchants, bought a few pots of petunias, and passed on the monster-sized sweet rolls slathered in thick cream cheese frosting, opting for fresh-squeezed orange juice instead. Here it was, seven thirty in the morning, and the smell of roasted corn reminded me of why I love coming down to the market. The food, flowers, and interesting people with their constant, quiet chatter. The white tents and long tables filled with silver jewelry, glazed clay pots, and tie-dyed shirts. It all made up the feel of a free open-air street festival, even in the rain.

I was a little soggy by the time I headed back to the car, laden with flowerpots and a few jars of cinnamon-spiced honey. Because the market wasn't as busy, the merchants had cut their prices, so I bought batches of flowers for a song. As I drove home, the inside of my car smelled like fresh-cut peonies and grass. The rain began to let up, and I could tell the rest of the day would be beautiful, the way it always is when the sun comes out after the rain. That thought, combined with my peaceful morning at the market, was a nice little pocket of joy. If happiness is dancing in the rain, joy is defying it.

It's all around us, in every season. In the summer, lush green grass and placid, glass-like lakes reflecting a powder blue, golden-lit sky. In the fall, panoramic mosaics of golds and yellows with the changing leaves. In the winter, pristine white snow made up of individual snowflakes that twinkle like jewels in the sunlight. And in the spring, soft gentle rain that washes away the old and makes way for the new.

It's all around us, if we look for it. The sunrise or sunset. The sleepy child with bedhead stealing your pillow. The cool breeze coming through the screened window. Yes, even the cliché smells of fresh-cut grass and fresh-brewed coffee. Finding your keys. Holding hands. The warm breath and soft kiss of the love of your life. Taking your heels off. Crying it all out. The funny way toddlers misplace syllables and consonants. Food of any sort, so long as it's your favorite. A yard sprinkler and the neighbor's kids. Sleeping in. Getting up and out after too many dark days of not being able to. Reunions. Embraces. Winning. Healing. Hoping. Saying yes to "Are we there yet?" Or any time anyone ever says yes . . . or no, depending on the question asked. The sound of children singing when they think no one is listening. Eating when you're hungry. Warmth when you're cold. Compassion when your heart aches.

There's no denying life gets messy and hard. We, as human beings, are a flawed, fallible bunch. Sometimes we get it right; sometimes we don't. Yet if the very axis of human engagement hinges on the balance between heartache and happiness, which will you choose to see?

I challenge you—rather, invite you—to look for and find the joy. Just as I did that Saturday morning in the rain.

That's why I've created this journal, just for you.

I believe joy is ever present, and while you may not find it every day, when you do, jot it down.

What was the date? Who were you with? Maybe you were all by yourself. That's okay too. What was your pocket of joy? However great or small. If the day had a hashtag, what would it be?

#Grateful
#Sunshine
#Home
#Love
#ItsGonnaBeOkay

In my first book, *Pockets of Joy: Deciding to Be Happy, Choosing to Be Free*, I wrote about being able to recognize those small moments of happiness that occur amidst life's difficult moments. I told stories of how I raised my son alone as a divorced single mom working a demanding television job. When my director of publishing, Lily Coyle, saw my manuscript for the first time, she noted how easy it would have been to write a "woe is me" story. She told me those are the types of stories she sees all the time and how it was so refreshing to see a memoir that focused on, of all things, joy.

As reader feedback started to come in, I was moved to hear how the book had inspired people to find joy in various life situations. A relative who was estranged from close family members, carrying a heavy burden of grief for years, vowed to let go of the hurt and move on with her life. A woman who had tragically lost her adult son gave it to her pregnant daughter-in-law to help her cope with raising a child who would never know his dad. I heard story after story from people who appreciated the reminder to "be happy on purpose" and, as one reader put it, "to look for moments of joy in the places God intended us to find them."

I encourage you to take a few moments to fill these pages with your own pockets of joy. Start by taking a moment to write down a time, however fleeting, when you were, of all things, happy. Be intentional about it. Remember what the day felt like and where you were. Be intentional about seeing and remembering joy.

Maybe you're thinking that's what social media is for. But think about it—by taking a few moments over time to write journal entries, rather than a series of tweets and posts that would be absorbed into some bottomless cybersphere, you will collect lasting memories of joy that have occurred in your life. Whether they be tiny eruptions or big sloppy splashes, the joy is, and forever will be, all yours.

I'm looking for inspiring stories for my next book,
so if you've got a pocket of joy you'd like to share,
e-mail me at roxane@roxanebattle.com.

Or if something good happens on the fly,
tweet it with the hashtag #pocketsofjoy.

THE DATE: _____ THE TIME: _____

THE PLACE: _____

I WAS WITH: _____

_____

MY POCKET OF JOY: _____

_____

_____

_____

_____

_____

_____

_____

_____

_____

_____

_____

_____

_____

_____

_____

_____

_____

_____

_____

_____

_____

_____

You will show me the path of life;
*in Your presence is fullness of **joy**,*
at Your right hand are pleasures
forevermore.

Psalm 16:11 (AMP)

_____

_____

_____

_____

_____

_____

_____

_____

_____

_____

_____

_____

_____

_____

_____

_____

_____

_____

TODAY'S #HASHTAG: _____

THE DATE: _____ THE TIME: _____

THE PLACE: _____

I WAS WITH: _____

_____

MY POCKET OF JOY: _____

_____

_____

_____

_____

_____

_____

_____

_____

_____

_____

_____

_____

_____

_____

_____

_____

_____

TODAY'S #HASHTAG:_____

THE DATE: _____ THE TIME: _____

THE PLACE: _____

I WAS WITH: _____

_____

MY POCKET OF JOY: _____

_____

_____

_____

_____

_____

_____

_____

_____

_____

_____

_____

_____

The Lord strengthens and protects me;
I trust in him with all my heart.
*I am rescued and my heart is full of **joy**;*
I will sing to him in gratitude.

Psalms 28:7 (NET)

TODAY'S #HASHTAG:_____

THE DATE: _____ THE TIME: _____

THE PLACE: _____

I WAS WITH: _____

_____

MY POCKET OF JOY: _____

_____

_____

_____

_____

_____

_____

_____

_____

_____

_____

_____

_____

_____

_____

_____

TODAY'S #HASHTAG:_____

THE DATE: _____ THE TIME: _____

THE PLACE: _____

I WAS WITH: _____

_____

MY POCKET OF JOY: _____

_____

_____

_____

_____

_____

_____

_____

_____

_____

_____

_____

_____

_____

_____

I pray that God, the source of hope,
*will fill you completely with **joy***
and peace because you trust in him.

Romans 15:13 (NLT)

_____

_____

_____

_____

_____

_____

_____

_____

_____

_____

_____

_____

_____

_____

_____

_____

_____

_____

_____

_____

TODAY'S #HASHTAG:_____

THE DATE: _____   THE TIME: _____

THE PLACE: _____

I WAS WITH: _____

_____

MY POCKET OF JOY: _____

_____

_____

_____

_____

_____

_____

_____

_____

_____

_____

_____

_____

_____

_____

_____

TODAY'S #HASHTAG: _____

THE DATE: _____ THE TIME: _____

THE PLACE: _____

I WAS WITH: _____

_____

MY POCKET OF JOY: _____

_____

_____

_____

_____

_____

_____

_____

_____

_____

_____

_____

_____

_____

_____

_____

_____

_____   *You will live in **joy** and peace.*

_____   Isaiah 55:12 (NLT)

TODAY'S #HASHTAG: _____

THE DATE: _____   THE TIME: _____

THE PLACE: _____

I WAS WITH: _____

_____

MY POCKET OF JOY: _____

_____

_____

_____

_____

_____

_____

_____

_____

_____

_____

_____

_____

_____

_____

_____

_____

TODAY'S #HASHTAG:_____

THE DATE: _____   THE TIME: _____

THE PLACE: _____

I WAS WITH: _____

_____

MY POCKET OF JOY: _____

_____

_____

_____

_____

_____

_____

_____

_____

_____

_____

_____

_____

_____

_____

_____

_____

He will yet fill your mouth with laughter
and your lips with shouts of **joy**.

Job 8:21 (TLB)

TODAY'S #HASHTAG:

THE DATE: _____   THE TIME: _____

THE PLACE: _____

I WAS WITH: _____

_____

MY POCKET OF JOY: _____

_____

_____

_____

_____

_____

_____

_____

_____

_____

_____

_____

_____

_____

_____

_____

_____

TODAY'S #HASHTAG:_____

THE DATE: _____ THE TIME: _____

THE PLACE: _____

I WAS WITH: _____

_____

MY POCKET OF JOY: _____

_____

_____

_____

_____

_____

_____

_____

_____

_____

_____

_____

_____

_____

Those who look to him for help will be   _____
*radiant with **joy**; no shadow of shame*   _____
will darken their faces.

Psalm 34:5 (NLT)   _____

TODAY'S #HASHTAG: _____

THE DATE: _____ THE TIME: _____

THE PLACE: _____

I WAS WITH: _____

_____

MY POCKET OF JOY: _____

_____

_____

_____

_____

_____

_____

_____

_____

_____

_____

_____

_____

_____

_____

_____

_____

_____

_____

_____

_____

_____

_____

_____

_____

_____

_____

_____

_____

_____

_____

_____

_____

_____

_____

_____

_____

TODAY'S #HASHTAG:_____

THE DATE: _____ THE TIME: _____

THE PLACE: _____

I WAS WITH: _____

_____

MY POCKET OF JOY: _____

_____

_____

_____

_____

_____

_____

_____

_____

_____

_____

_____

_____

_____

_____

_____

God's laws are perfect. They protect us,
*make us wise, and give us **joy** and light*

Psalm 19:8 (TLB)

_____

_____

_____

_____

_____

_____

_____

_____

_____

_____

_____

_____

_____

_____

_____

_____

_____

_____

_____

_____

_____

TODAY'S #HASHTAG: _____

THE DATE: _____ THE TIME: _____

THE PLACE: _____

I WAS WITH: _____

_____

MY POCKET OF JOY: _____

_____

_____

_____

_____

_____

_____

_____

_____

_____

_____

_____

_____

_____

_____

_____

TODAY'S #HASHTAG:_____

THE DATE: _____   THE TIME: _____

THE PLACE: _____

I WAS WITH: _____

_____

MY POCKET OF JOY: _____

_____

_____

_____

_____

_____

_____

_____

_____

_____

_____

_____

_____

_____

_____

_____   *The hope of the righteous brings **joy**.*

_____   Proverbs 10:28 (ESV)

TODAY'S #HASHTAG:_____

THE DATE: _____ THE TIME: _____

THE PLACE: _____

I WAS WITH: _____

_____

MY POCKET OF JOY: _____

_____

_____

_____

_____

_____

_____

_____

_____

_____

_____

_____

_____

_____

_____

_____

_____

_____

TODAY'S #HASHTAG: _____

THE DATE: _____   THE TIME: _____

THE PLACE: _____

I WAS WITH: _____

_____

MY POCKET OF JOY: _____

_____

_____

_____

_____

_____

_____

_____

_____

_____

_____

_____

_____

_____

_____

_____

_____

_____

_____

_____

_____

Up to now, you have asked nothing in my name.
Ask and you will receive so that
*your **joy** will be complete.*

John 16:24 (CEB)

TODAY'S #HASHTAG: _____

THE DATE: _____ THE TIME: _____

THE PLACE: _____

I WAS WITH: _____

_____

MY POCKET OF JOY: _____

_____

_____

_____

_____

_____

_____

_____

_____

_____

_____

_____

_____

_____

_____

_____

_____

_____

_____

_____

_____

_____

_____

_____

_____

_____

_____

_____

_____

_____

_____

_____

_____

_____

_____

_____

_____

_____

_____

TODAY'S #HASHTAG: _____

THE DATE: _____ THE TIME: _____

THE PLACE: _____

I WAS WITH: _____

_____

MY POCKET OF JOY: _____

_____

_____

_____

_____

_____

_____

_____

_____

_____

_____

_____

_____

*The fruit of the Spirit is, love, **joy**,*
peace, patience, kindness, goodness,
faithfulness, gentleness, and self-control.
There is no law against things like this.

Galatians 5:22-23 (CEB)

_____

_____

_____

_____

TODAY'S #HASHTAG:_____

THE DATE: _____   THE TIME: _____

THE PLACE: _____

I WAS WITH: _____

_____

MY POCKET OF JOY: _____

_____

_____

_____

_____

_____

_____

_____

_____

_____

_____

_____

_____

_____

_____

_____

_____

TODAY'S #HASHTAG: _____

THE DATE: _____ THE TIME: _____

THE PLACE: _____

I WAS WITH: _____

_____

MY POCKET OF JOY: _____

_____

_____

_____

_____

_____

_____

_____

_____

_____

_____

_____

_____

_____

_____

_____

*Those who sow tears shall reap **joy**.*

Psalms 126:5 (TLB)

_____   _____

_____   _____

_____

_____

_____

_____

_____

_____

_____

_____

_____

_____

_____

_____

_____

_____

_____

_____

_____

_____

_____

_____

TODAY'S #HASHTAG: _____

THE DATE: _____   THE TIME: _____

THE PLACE: _____

I WAS WITH: _____

_____

MY POCKET OF JOY: _____

_____

_____

_____

_____

_____

_____

_____

_____

_____

_____

_____

_____

_____

_____

_____

_____

_____

_____

_____

_____

_____

_____

_____

_____

_____

_____

_____

_____

_____

_____

_____

_____

_____

_____

_____

_____

_____

_____

_____

TODAY'S #HASHTAG:_____

THE DATE: _____   THE TIME: _____

THE PLACE: _____

I WAS WITH: _____

_____

MY POCKET OF JOY: _____

_____

_____

_____

_____

_____

_____

_____

_____

_____

_____

_____

_____

_____   *Light shines on the godly, and **joy**
                                    on those whose hearts are right.*

_____   Psalm 97:11 (NLT)

_____

TODAY'S #HASHTAG:_____

THE DATE: _____ THE TIME: _____

THE PLACE: _____

I WAS WITH: _____

_____

MY POCKET OF JOY: _____

_____

_____

_____

_____

_____

_____

_____

_____

_____

_____

_____

_____

_____

_____

_____

_____

TODAY'S #HASHTAG:

THE DATE: _____   THE TIME: _____

THE PLACE: _____

I WAS WITH: _____

_____

MY POCKET OF JOY: _____

_____

_____

_____

_____

_____

_____

_____

_____

_____

_____

_____

_____

_____

_____

_____

_____

_____

_____

_____

God gives wisdom, knowledge,
*and **joy** to those who please Him.*

Ecclesiastes 2:26 (NLT)

_____

_____

_____

_____

_____

_____

_____

_____

_____

_____

_____

_____

_____

_____

_____

_____

_____

_____

TODAY'S #HASHTAG: _____

THE DATE: _____ THE TIME: _____

THE PLACE: _____

I WAS WITH: _____

_____

MY POCKET OF JOY: _____

_____

_____

_____

_____

_____

_____

_____

_____

_____

_____

_____

_____

_____

_____

_____

_____

TODAY'S #HASHTAG:_____

THE DATE: _____   THE TIME: _____

THE PLACE: _____

I WAS WITH: _____

_____

MY POCKET OF JOY: _____

_____

_____

_____

_____

_____

_____

_____

_____

_____

_____

_____

_____

You will give me back my life and give   _____
*me wonderful **joy** in your presence.*   _____

Acts 2:28 (TLB)   _____

                                                _____

_____

_____

_____

_____

_____

_____

_____

_____

_____

_____

_____

_____

_____

_____

_____

_____

_____

_____

_____

_____

_____

_____

TODAY'S #HASHTAG:_____

THE DATE: _____ THE TIME: _____

THE PLACE: _____

I WAS WITH: _____

_____

MY POCKET OF JOY: _____

_____

_____

_____

_____

_____

_____

_____

_____

_____

_____

_____

_____

_____

_____

_____

_____

TODAY'S #HASHTAG:_____

THE DATE: _____   THE TIME: _____

THE PLACE: _____

I WAS WITH: _____

_____

MY POCKET OF JOY: _____

_____

_____

_____

_____

_____

_____

_____

_____

_____

_____

_____

_____

_____

_____

_____

Weeping may endure for a night,
*but **joy** comes in the morning.*

Psalm 30:5 (NKJV)

TODAY'S #HASHTAG: _____

THE DATE: _____ THE TIME: _____

THE PLACE: _____

I WAS WITH: _____

_____

MY POCKET OF JOY: _____

_____

_____

_____

_____

_____

_____

_____

_____

_____

_____

_____

_____

_____

_____

_____

_____

_____

_____

_____

_____

_____

_____

_____

_____

_____

_____

_____

_____

_____

_____

_____

_____

_____

_____

_____

_____

TODAY'S #HASHTAG:_____

THE DATE: _____ THE TIME: _____

THE PLACE: _____

I WAS WITH: _____

_____

MY POCKET OF JOY: _____

_____

_____

_____

_____

_____

_____

_____

_____

_____

_____

_____

_____

_____

_____

_____

_____

Think of the various tests you
*encounter as occasions for **joy**.*
After all, you know that the testing of
your faith produces endurance.

James 1:2–3 (CEB)

TODAY'S #HASHTAG:_____

THE DATE: _____ THE TIME: _____

THE PLACE: _____

I WAS WITH: _____

_____

MY POCKET OF JOY: _____

_____

_____

_____

_____

_____

_____

_____

_____

_____

_____

_____

_____

_____

_____

_____

TODAY'S #HASHTAG: _____

THE DATE: _____ THE TIME: _____

THE PLACE: _____

I WAS WITH: _____

_____

MY POCKET OF JOY: _____

_____

_____

_____

_____

_____

_____

_____

_____

_____

_____

_____

_____

_____

_____

_____

_____

Clap your hands, all peoples!
*Shout to God with loud songs of **joy**!*

Psalm 47:1 (ESV)

_____

_____

_____

_____

_____

_____

_____

_____

_____

_____

_____

_____

_____

_____

_____

_____

_____

_____

_____

_____

TODAY'S #HASHTAG:_____

THE DATE: _____   THE TIME: _____

THE PLACE: _____

I WAS WITH: _____

_____

MY POCKET OF JOY: _____

_____

_____

_____

_____

_____

_____

_____

_____

_____

_____

_____

_____

_____

_____

_____

_____

_____

_____

_____

_____

_____

_____

_____

_____

_____

_____

_____

_____

_____

_____

_____

_____

_____

_____

_____

_____

_____

_____

TODAY'S #HASHTAG:_____

THE DATE: _____   THE TIME: _____

THE PLACE: _____

I WAS WITH: _____

_____

MY POCKET OF JOY: _____

_____

_____

_____

_____

_____

_____

_____

_____

_____

_____

_____

_____

_____

_____

*Your love has given me great **joy**
and encouragement.*
Philemon 1:7 (NIV)

_____

_____

_____

_____

_____

_____

_____

_____

_____

_____

_____

_____

_____

_____

_____

_____

_____

_____

_____

_____

_____

_____

_____

_____

TODAY'S #HASHTAG:_____

THE DATE: _____   THE TIME: _____

THE PLACE: _____

I WAS WITH: _____

_____

MY POCKET OF JOY: _____

_____

_____

_____

_____

_____

_____

_____

_____

_____

_____

_____

_____

_____

_____

_____

_____

_____

_____

_____

_____

_____

_____

_____

_____

_____

_____

_____

_____

_____

_____

_____

_____

_____

_____

_____

TODAY'S #HASHTAG: _____

THE DATE: _____   THE TIME: _____

THE PLACE: _____

I WAS WITH: _____

_____

MY POCKET OF JOY: _____

_____

_____

_____

_____

_____

_____

_____

_____

_____

_____

_____

_____

_____

_____

_____

*Sorrow and mourning will disappear,
and they will be filled with **joy**
and gladness.*

Isaiah 35:10 (NLT)

_____

_____

_____

_____

_____

_____

_____

_____

_____

_____

_____

_____

_____

_____

_____

_____

_____

_____

_____

_____

_____

_____

TODAY'S #HASHTAG: _____

THE DATE: _____   THE TIME: _____

THE PLACE: _____

I WAS WITH: _____

_____

MY POCKET OF JOY: _____

_____

_____

_____

_____

_____

_____

_____

_____

_____

_____

_____

_____

_____

_____

_____

_____

_____

_____

_____

_____

_____

_____

_____

_____

_____

_____

_____

_____

_____

_____

_____

_____

_____

_____

_____

TODAY'S #HASHTAG:_____

THE DATE: _____   THE TIME: _____

THE PLACE: _____

I WAS WITH: _____

_____

MY POCKET OF JOY: _____

_____

_____

_____

_____

_____

_____

_____

_____

_____

_____

_____

_____

_____

_____

_____   *A person finds **joy** in giving an apt reply—*
                          and how good is a timely word!

_____   Proverbs 15:23 (NIV)

TODAY'S #HASHTAG:_____

THE DATE: _____   THE TIME: _____

THE PLACE: _____

I WAS WITH: _____

_____

MY POCKET OF JOY: _____

_____

_____

_____

_____

_____

_____

_____

_____

_____

_____

_____

_____

_____

_____

_____

_____

TODAY'S #HASHTAG:_____

THE DATE: _____   THE TIME: _____

THE PLACE: _____

I WAS WITH: _____

_____

MY POCKET OF JOY: _____

_____

_____

_____

_____

_____

_____

_____

_____

_____

_____

_____

_____

_____

_____

_____

When I see you again, you'll be full of **joy**, and it will be a joy no one can rob from you.

John 16:22 (MSG)

TODAY'S #HASHTAG:

THE DATE: _____   THE TIME: _____

THE PLACE: _____

I WAS WITH: _____

_____

MY POCKET OF JOY: _____

_____

_____

_____

_____

_____

_____

_____

_____

_____

_____

_____

_____

_____

_____

_____

TODAY'S #HASHTAG:_____

THE DATE: _____ THE TIME: _____

THE PLACE: _____

I WAS WITH: _____

_____

MY POCKET OF JOY: _____

_____

_____

_____

_____

_____

_____

_____

_____

_____

_____

_____

God's kingdom isn't a matter of what
you put in your stomach, for goodness'
sake. It's what God does with your life
as he sets it right, puts it together,
*and completes it with **joy**.*

Romans 14:17 (MSG)

TODAY'S #HASHTAG:_____

THE DATE: _____   THE TIME: _____

THE PLACE: _____

I WAS WITH: _____

_____

MY POCKET OF JOY: _____

_____

_____

_____

_____

_____

_____

_____

_____

_____

_____

_____

_____

_____

_____

_____

_____

TODAY'S #HASHTAG:

THE DATE: _____   THE TIME: _____

THE PLACE: _____

I WAS WITH: _____

_____

MY POCKET OF JOY: _____

_____

_____

_____

_____

_____

_____

_____

_____

_____

_____

_____

_____

_____

_____

_____

_____

Majestic splendor emanates from him,
*he is the source of strength and **joy**.*

1 Chronicles 16:27 (NET)

_____

_____

_____

_____

_____

_____

_____

_____

_____

_____

_____

_____

_____

_____

_____

_____

_____

_____

_____

_____

_____

_____

TODAY'S #HASHTAG:_____

THE DATE: _____ THE TIME: _____

THE PLACE: _____

I WAS WITH: _____

_____

MY POCKET OF JOY: _____

_____

_____

_____

_____

_____

_____

_____

_____

_____

_____

_____

_____

_____

_____

_____

TODAY'S #HASHTAG:_____

THE DATE: _____   THE TIME: _____

THE PLACE: _____

I WAS WITH: _____

_____

MY POCKET OF JOY: _____

_____

_____

_____

_____

_____

_____

_____

_____

_____

_____

_____

_____

_____

_____   *The **joy** of the Lord*
                                    is your strength.

_____   Nehemiah 8:10 (ESV)

_____

_____

_____

_____

_____

_____

_____

_____

_____

_____

_____

_____

_____

_____

_____

_____

_____

_____

_____

_____

_____

_____

_____

TODAY'S #HASHTAG:_____

THE DATE: _____   THE TIME: _____

THE PLACE: _____

I WAS WITH: _____

_____

MY POCKET OF JOY: _____

_____

_____

_____

_____

_____

_____

_____

_____

_____

_____

_____

_____

_____

_____

_____

_____

_____

TODAY'S #HASHTAG:_____

THE DATE: _____   THE TIME: _____

THE PLACE: _____

I WAS WITH: _____

_____

MY POCKET OF JOY: _____

_____

_____

_____

_____

_____

_____

_____

_____

_____

_____

_____

_____

_____

_____

_____

_____

_____

_____

_____

*Grant me the ultimate **joy**
of being forgiven!*

Psalm 51:8 (NET)

_____

_____

_____

_____

_____

_____

_____

_____

_____

_____

_____

_____

_____

_____

_____

_____

_____

_____

_____

TODAY'S #HASHTAG:_____

THE DATE: _____   THE TIME: _____

THE PLACE: _____

I WAS WITH: _____

_____

MY POCKET OF JOY: _____

_____

_____

_____

_____

_____

_____

_____

_____

_____

_____

_____

_____

_____

_____

_____

_____

TODAY'S #HASHTAG:_____

THE DATE: _____   THE TIME: _____

THE PLACE: _____

I WAS WITH: _____

_____

MY POCKET OF JOY: _____

_____

_____

_____

_____

_____

_____

_____

_____

_____

_____

_____

_____

_____

I claim your rules as my permanent   _____
*possession for they give me **joy**.*
                                              _____
Psalm 119:111 (NET)
                                              _____

TODAY'S #HASHTAG:_____

THE DATE: _____ THE TIME: _____

THE PLACE: _____

I WAS WITH: _____

_____

MY POCKET OF JOY: _____

_____

_____

_____

_____

_____

_____

_____

_____

_____

_____

_____

_____

_____

_____

_____

_____

_____

TODAY'S #HASHTAG:

THE DATE: _____ THE TIME: _____

THE PLACE: _____

I WAS WITH: _____

_____

MY POCKET OF JOY: _____

_____

_____

_____

_____

_____

_____

_____

_____

_____

_____

_____

_____

_____

_____

_____

_____

*A twinkle in the eye means **joy** in the heart and good news makes you feel fit as a fiddle.*

Proverbs 15:30 (MSG)

_____

_____

_____

_____

_____

_____

_____

_____

_____

_____

_____

_____

_____

_____

_____

_____

_____

_____

_____

_____

TODAY'S #HASHTAG: _____

THE DATE: _____ THE TIME: _____

THE PLACE: _____

I WAS WITH: _____

_____

MY POCKET OF JOY: _____

_____

_____

_____

_____

_____

_____

_____

_____

_____

_____

_____

_____

_____

_____

_____

TODAY'S #HASHTAG:

THE DATE: _____   THE TIME: _____

THE PLACE: _____

I WAS WITH: _____

_____

MY POCKET OF JOY: _____

_____

_____

_____

_____

_____

_____

_____

_____

_____

_____

_____

_____

_____

_____

_____   *Looking to Jesus, the founder and*
*perfecter of our faith, who for the **joy***
_____   *that was set before him endured the*
cross, despising the shame, and is seated
_____   *at the right hand of the throne of God.*

_____   Hebrews 12:2 (ESV)

TODAY'S #HASHTAG:

"Pockets of joy—those fleeting moments when you feel like everything is going to be okay."
—Roxane Battle

EPILOGUE

CONGRATULATIONS! You did it. You took time to recount the joy in your life and to intentionally celebrate that happiness can be found. Good job! You now have your very own pocket of joy, a collection of happy memories to look back on and remember during the moments when joy may be hard to find.

You are now officially part of the **#pocketsofjoy** movement! Together we can spread even more joy. How? So glad you asked. I'm thrilled to let you know I'm working on a follow-up to *Pockets of Joy: Deciding to Be Happy, Choosing to Be Free*, and this time it's all about you.

Now that you've collected your stories, is there one you'd like to share? I'd love to read about the gleeful, spontaneous moments in your life, or the things you learned to get you through the tough times. What makes you happy, and how'd you get there? Think about it—together we can create ripples of joy that know no end.

Send your stories to roxane@roxanebattle.com. You'll receive an e-mail confirmation directly from me if your story is selected for publication in my next book. Thanks so much!

Joyfully,

Roxane Battle

ISBN-13: 978-1-59298-848-8